OUT ON A LEASH